Sukarno and the idea of Indonesia

A history of Indonesian nationalism

Sukarno
and the idea of Indonesia

A history of Indonesian nationalism

A book by Axel Weber

Bibliografische Information der Deutschen Nationalbibliothek: Die Deutsche Nationalbibliothek verzeichnet diese Publikation in der Deutschen Nationalbibliografie; detaillierte bibliografische Daten sind im Internet über dnb.dnb.de abrufbar.

Herstellung und Verlag: BoD – Books on Demand, Norderstedt

ISBN: 9783751960748

Table of contents

The perspective

This book was originally written as an essay for my studies at the Ludwig-Maximilians University in Munich. I was majoring in political sciences and had chosen anthropology as one of the two minor subjects. That was sixteen years ago. Back then I was immersing myself in the history of Indonesia. My studies took me into the analysis of the post-colonial state and the political imagination of emerging new nation states. During a number of sojourns in Indonesia I traveled to the historic places where Indonesia had built its modern identity: Lubang Buaya, the crocodile's pit, the place where the bodies of the seven generals were dumped on 30 September 1965; the Selamat Datang Monument on Bundaran H.I., the epicenter of the Indonesian nation; the Sarinah department store on Jl. Thamrin as well as the national monument Monas and the old town of Kota in Jakarta, the formerly Dutch Batavia. I sauntered down Pasar Baru and passed the offices of Antara, the Indonesian news agency. The old Hotel Indonesia with its huge swimming pool still existed. I walked down the avenues and major arteries of Jakarta named after the generals and freedom fighters mentioned in the following chapters. During my first stay in 2002 I rented a pavilion on Jl. Cianjur in Menteng, one of the most affluent and most centrally located neighborhoods of the capital city, ibu kota. The place was walking distance from Menteng Plaza and Bundaran H.I., even though I was the only one walking, Jakarta being a driver's city. Wherever I went, the smell of Jakarta was the same, and it was also the smell that welcomed you to the terminal building of Jakarta's Soekarno-Hatta International Airport: kretek, Indonesia's clove cigarettes. The guards of the mansions of the wealthy in Menteng would smoke kretek cigarettes, their blue smoke dissolving in the hot and humid air of Jakarta. Many times did I pass the well-guarded housing complex of Suharto, the nation's second President, in Menteng. When Suharto finally passed away in 2008 it was exciting to see in how far Indonesia would come to terms with its past and get some "Vergangenheitsbewältigung" done. Ten years earlier, when "krismon", the Indonesian abbreviation for "krisis moneter", the financial crisis of 1997-98, had helped bring down Suharto and his regime after 31 years in power, the world held its breath, unsure if the country would make a peaceful transition into a Western model of democracy, or whether the archipelago would fall into a bloody civil war and ethnic cleansing, as it had when Suharto had come to power. Suharto murdered, killed and incarcerated millions of his own people, and he embezzled billions of dollars during his reign, while the West looked away. The CIA had lifted Suharto into power to create a devote regime as bulwark against the advance of communism from within and without. Sukarno's flirt with the East was unacceptable to the West, and as in many other places around the world, it was better to have a brutal yet West-leaning dictator in power, a so-called puppet, than to accept a nation's freedom of choice. "We have to remember that the genocide, the military dictatorship which followed (after Sukarno), the present day impunity for gangsters and thugs and the use of them by corporations and by the government, this is the West's vision for Indonesia, and for many places like Indonesia," says Joshua Oppenheimer.[1] Suharto's dictatorship lasted for more than 30 years, and cost Indonesia much of the freedom envisioned by Sukarno. Not only was corruption rampant, but a whole new system was in place: KKN. KKN is short for *korupsi, kolusi, nepotisme*, in English corruption, collusion and nepotism. To this very day Indonesians use KKN as a verb or noun to describe the unlawful making-it happen of something that would otherwise never have happened, or would have taken ages.[2] Even though Suharto promised to fight KKN, he and his regime thrived on KKN, were the machine behind it. The dictator and his inner circle and family benefited from selling out his country to Western powers and corporations

---

[1] Joshua Oppenheimer in "Joshua Oppenheimer on "The Act of Killing": The VICE Podcast 034."

[2] I came into contact with KKN the first time when my wife and I tried to visit the upstairs observation platform on Monas in rain on my final day in the city. The platform was slippery and closed during the rainy season. My friend said, "Give me 100,000 rupiah, and I will get us in." Back in 2002, this was about EUR 6,- The guard was very happy to give us a private tour of the observation deck. The second time worth mentioning here was when the immigration officer at the airport prevented me from leaving the country as I had, in his eyes, overstayed my visa by 24 hours. I had 30 minutes to boarding, and no time to argue. I was more callous then, and asked him "How much does it cost me to catch my plane?" It turned out that he wanted USD 90. I only had rupiah on myself, and I raised my voice that when he wanted USD there was an exchange booth nearby. I paid up in rupiah and left the country. Cheaper than having to book a new flight. But symptomatic for Indonesia. Another time worth mentioning was when I drove my wife's car through a red light at the pizza man statue, officially the Patung Pemuda Membangun, and the police man could not decide what to do with my EU driver's licence, so he decided to keep my wife's licence. He wanted EUR 10,- to make it all go away. My wife refused and we drove on to get a new driver's licence for my wife. KKN is everywhere in Indonesia, and sadly enough, it makes the place function.

- KKN on the highest level. With the CIA backing Suharto, the West gave Suharto a carte blanche to kill and plunder his own people and their property, under the pretext of defending Indonesia against a Communist threat. This had been the CIA's third attempt to change the political landscape in Indonesia. First, one of the CIA pilots sent in a B-26 bomber in 1958 to help a rebellion of certain parts of the Indonesian military had embarrassingly been shut down and captured. And secondly a ruse to bring the Muslim Sukarno down with a fake porn movie, shot in Hollywood featuring the President himself, could not bring the Indonesian people nor the establishment to abandon Sukarno.

Against the background of the developments of the second half of the 20th century the unique story of the birth of the fourth largest and most populous Muslim country in the world is often forgotten and overlooked. Pramoedya Ananta Toer, one of Indonesia's foremost writers, wrote in 1999 that "Sukarno was the only Asian leader of the modern era able to unify people of such differing ethnic, cultural and religious backgrounds without shedding a drop of blood."[3] This could not contrast stronger with his successor who had to use extreme violence to consolidate his power, called "The New Order." Sukarno was a President of the people for the people. The independence movement and nation building happened mainly during the final phase of the Dutch era as well as the Japanese occupation of the islands during the Second World War. Only two days passed between the surrender

---

3 http://edition.cnn.com/ASIANOW/time/asia/magazine/1999/990823/sukarno1.html

of the Japanese Tenno and the Declaration of Independence of Indonesia on 17 August 1945. Yet another five years had to pass before the last of the Dutch political structures were dissolved; the Dutch had officially recognised Indonesian independence only in 1949 under pressure from the UN and the international community. There were more Europeans killed in the guerilla and resistance battles after the end the World War II then during the war. So fierce were the Indonesians, so weak the Dutch. It was a predecessor that showed that no Western nation would be able to win a guerilla war in Asia.

The becoming of Indonesia is a prime example of nationalistic studies in colonised territories. By sheer size this archipelago dwarfs all the other nine member states of the ASEAN as well as most other nations world wide. We can only guess at what would have happened had Sukarno remained in power and had the failed coup by the 30 September Movement (*G30S PKI, Gerakan 30 September PKI*) and counter coup of the military in 1965 never taken place - or had the outcome been different. Instead of speculating about what could have been, the last part of the book focuses on the harsh reality after Sukarno's demise, when Suharto took over power in Jakarta and diminished much of the freedom Sukarno had envisioned, as well as been fighting for. Sukarno, the *dalang*, the puppet master who for a long time had balanced the PKI and the military against each other, especially during the last period of the Guided Democracy, had failed at restoring his regime after the developments of 30 September and was subsequently put under house arrest. Suharto became acting President in March 1967, and was officially appointed President one year later. *Bung Karno*, older brother Karno, as he was lovingly called by his people, died on 21 June 1970.

I have included most if not all the books and sources I used for research. The argument of the final chapter is based on John Pilger's in his very convincing book "The New Rulers of the World". The main outline of his book has been turned into a movie[4] worth watching, not only for context. Pilger's argument focuses on how the West and its mighty corporations have enslaved the newly independent and emerging economies like Indonesia. Suharto was a willing actor and puppet in this charade. Sukarno's bold move to help form the Non-Aligned Movement (NAM) during the Bandung Conference of 1955 can be seen as one way of transporting his idea of Pancasila into an international context. The aim of the NAM was to end dominance of one country over another, promote international cooperation, peace and especially independence of emerging countries from their former oppressors in a world which became ever more bipolar during the Cold War.

Sukarno's nationalism carries a strong visual component. Sukarno was a master speaker in seven languages. While his opponents accused him of having become a demagogue, he willingly employed his powers of speech to the benefit of his nation. I found some works of historical fiction a fascinating source to complement my picture of Indonesia in the final phase of Sukarno's power. First and foremost Christopher Koch's book "The Year of Living Dangerously", which has also been turned

[4] http://johnpilger.com/videos/the-new-rulers-of-the-world

into a movie with Mel Gibson and Sigourney Weaver in the lead roles and which won Linda Hunt an academy award for best supporting actress as the male Billy Kwan. The movie was banned in Indonesia until the year 2000. In my eyes this book is to Indonesia what Graham Greene's "The Quiet American" is to Vietnam. Then there are the novels by Kerry B. Collison, first and foremost "The Timor Man" and "Merdeka Square", which I picked up in the QB World Bookshop off Thamrin, while it still existed. These texts paint a realistic picture of an era gone by, but are forever embedded in our minds as the final and happy days of a virgin Indonesia.

This book is in parts focusing on an academic documentation of its argument, but is not striving to be an academic work in itself. This perspective would be incomplete if I did not declare my admiration for the Wayang Sukarno used to build his nation, nor the way Hindu, Buddhist as well as Muslim concepts found their way into the political arena of the Indonesian reality.

Frankfurt am Main, 2020

Indonesia and nationalism

According to the number of its inhabitants, Indonesia is the fourth largest nation on the planet. The sheer number of diverse minorities as well as geographic, ethnic, linguistic, religious and political differences makes it unique.[5] This multi-ethnic and multi-island state is home and *Vaterland* to a huge number of ethnicities and this makes Indonesia a babylonic archipelago.[6] For these reasons, this huge island nation, located between the Indian and Pacific oceans, is constantly fighting against the disrupture of its sovereign territory.[7] The biggest trouble-maker to the central government in Jakarta is the province *Nanggroe Aceh Darussalam* (NAD), or in short Aceh, located on the northern tip of the island of Sumatra. Aceh has never formally accepted the Dutch colonial government nor the Indonesian government and its desire for independence is a factor of instability for Indonesia.

West Papua, in the very east of the country (and more than 5,000 KM from Aceh) poses a similar threat. The local minorities feel exploited by the Jakarta elites who, since Suharto took over power, have been in cahoots with the mostly western oil, gas and mining corporations. Since 1960, this conflict has killed more than 100,000 Papuans.[8] On the *Maluku Islands* (famous for their

[5] Strassner 1998, p.313.

[6] See Anderson, Benedict R. 2003, p.120ff.

[7] See Khalik 2003.

[8] The Jakarta Post Online 2004. General Moerdani dies at 74. August 29, 2004.

spices), Muslims are fighting Christians in their desire to create an islamic state. Indonesia's geographical identity is under attack by the secession of *East Timor* in 1999 and the de facto establishment as a nation in 2002. The government feared that other regions would hold referenda that might lead to independence. This again could create a momentum too strong to control for Jakarta. After a ruling in 2002 by the International Court of Justice (ICJ) Jakarta had to accept that the two islands *Sipadan* and *Ligitan*, who until then were Indonesian, were attributed to Malaysia. This directly entailed a trip of the then-president to the small and uninhabited island of *Nipah* near the border with Singapore. Even though this island is completely submerged during high tide, the Indonesian government installed a badge on the island clearly marking it as Indonesian territory.[9]

The current Indonesian president, Joko Widodo, is taking a stronger stand against the Chinese aggression in the South China Sea, which might be endangering the territorial sovereignty of the island nation from the north. Even though the Chinese government in Beijing is not disputing the *Natuna Islands* themselves, they do lay claim on the "nine-dash line" surrounding the islands, and hence create a conflict with Indonesia's 200-nautical-mile exclusive economic zone.[10]

Against the background of these centrifugal forces it is interesting to understand how Indonesia actually came into existence as a nation state, especially as the country did not exist

[9] See The Jakarta Post; regarding *Nipah* see: Unidjaja and Desy 2004.

[10] The Economist. July 2nd 2016. Indonesia and the South China Sea. Annoyed in Natuna.

as a political and administrative unit before the Dutch colonialism.[11]

This essay undertakes the task of investigating the central notions and thoughts that led to the territorial unity of Indonesia as a sovereign nation and its independence.

Indonesia is a prime example for studies of nationalism in postcolonial societies: since 1912 Java has been "the place of historically unprecedented independence movement."[12] Only with the example of Indonesia and especially Java can we understand what it means for a colonial territory to spread the ideas of independence and the nation state. The terms and the idea of unity were unknown to the peoples of the future Indonesia, spreading over 18,000 islands.

Even in the 1940s most of the *Marhaen*[13] did not know what the terms independence and state meant. An anecdote from Sukarno's biography beautifully proves the point:

> *„In 1946 and 1947 people didn't understand what a President's duties were. They also didn't understand exactly what independence meant. Following our declaration that everybody was free we had difficulty*

[11] Asian Forum for Human Rights and Development [FORUM-ASIA] (ed.) 1995, p.19.
[12] Dahm 1966, p.9.
[13] Marhaen is Sukarno's terminology for the rural proletariat. More below.

making the Marhaens pay passage in the tram carp. 'Why?' they'd cry with a hurt and bewildered look. 'We're free, aren't we?'"[14]

Sukarno, nation founder, first president and father of the former, female president Megawati Sukarnoputri, takes center stage in our investigation. Sukarno managed to unify the different drifts of independence and to steer them into the direction of a unified Indonesia. Next to quite a number of enigmatic and dazzling historic figures, who deserve to be mentioned in the context of independence and nation-building, it is Sukarno to whom the people of Indonesia are thankful the most. He provided them their *tanah air*, their "soil and water", their *Vaterland.*

The main reason why we devote most of our attention to Sukarno is the fact that he became the political philosopher of his country. He blended elements of Javanese mythology and history with notions of modern Islam and socialism. His terms and concepts of *marhaenism* and *pancasila* are strong expressions of this Indonesian political philosophy; *pancasila* is anchored in the constitution to this very day.

Sukmawati Soekarnoputri, daughter of Sukarno and sister of Megawati, joined the parliamentary elections in 2004 (even though with little success) with her newly founded party *Partai*

[14] Sukarno 1965, p.243.

Nasional Indonesia Marhaenisme (PNI Marhaenisme) by directly tying into her father's program.[15]

Many Indonesians were disillusioned by the corrupt regime of Suharto, Sukarno's successor. They were living with the uncertainty of where their country would be going after the fall of Suharto in 1998. The era of Sukarno as well as the person himself stand for a golden time in the history of their nation[16], just as the bygone *Majapahit* was for Sukarno.

To understand the political developments of today's Indonesia it is compelling to look into the past and to undertake an excursion into the history of nation-becoming of Indonesia.

---

[15] See The Jakarta Post Onlinc 2004. I am ready to become president, says Guruh Soekarnoputra. January 19, 2004.

[16] O'Rourke 2002, p.203f and Schwarz 1999, p.6.

Indonesia: idea and notion

First, let's have a look at the idea and notion of the newly created territorial state of Indonesia, and how the thought and the consciousness of the same came into being. Detached from history, we are going to look at some basic categories of the expression of the national state and investigate when and how they appeared. This will lend us a better understanding of the Indonesian state. We will also keep in mind that Java takes center stage within the Indonesian cosmos.

The notion of Indonesia was preceded by the notion of Java, and language hereby plays a special role. In 1917 the *java dipa* movement was founded to reform language. *Java dipa* means "uplifted Java". Its task was to rid the Javanese language of the "caste system" and to introduce the idea of equality. The most important aspect was to get rid of the *kawula-gusti*, the master-servant-relationship, dating back to the middle ages. Its concept was rooted in the idea that in a social setting people had to talk bottom to top *kromo*, and top to bottom *ngoko*. Javanese was a language of servility. With the *Sarekat Islam* (Islamic Union, SI) taking up this topic, the focus shifted in the 1920s away from Java towards the complete archipelago and created a new problem: Javanese was no adequate administrative language for all the other islands, of which there are plenty. Malay took up this role. Malay became "the weapon of the nationalists."[17] The

[17] Dahm 1966, p.28.

linguistic struggle went so far that the young chairman of SI and mentor as well as former father-in-law of Sukarno, Cokroaminoto, refused as early as 1913 during a meeting with the Dutch governor Idenburg to speak Dutch, even though Cokroaminoto was fluent in the language.[18] In the past Malay had served traders, then islam and finally the colonials as official tongue (*Dienstmaleiisch*).

It was crucial for the nationalists to use the same language, i.e. Malay and not Dutch; no social demarcation should be possible through the means of communication. In addition the problem of a common language across all islands was solved.[19] Even the independence movement of *West Papua*, OPM, made use of the Indonesian language for the purpose of their own nationalism (OPM, *Organisasi Papua Merdeka*).[20] Sukarno saw the advantages of the use of Bahasa Indonesia in terminating the linguistic separation not only but especially in Java, where social differences were exacerbated through Javanese. From now on young and old, rich and poor, president and farmer were able to use the same form of salutation. This “cultural revolution“ gave birth to the terms *Bapak*, *Ibu* and *Bung*. President Sukarno thus became Bung Karno, the brother of all citizens he aspired to be.[21]

Sukarno attributes immense pride to the success of the Indonesian language:

---

[18] See Dahm 1966, p.28 footnote 49.

[19] See Dahm 1966, p.27-28.

[20] OPM, *Organisasi Papua Merdeka*, means Organisation Free Papua. Anderson, Benedict R. O’G. 2003, p.178 footnote 27.

[21] See Sukarno 1965, p.73-74.

"And can I not justifiably express pride in the fact that whereas India is now battling over a unitary language and China has not yet a unitary language, my Marhaens, spread over 10,000 islands, all speak Bahasa Indonesia?"[22]

At the same time, Bahasa Indonesia became an intellectual vehicle, because the ethnically neutral language was used as a medium for literature and publications of all kind.[23] In 1922 Marah Roesli published the first Indonesian novel, *Sitti Noerbaja*.[24] The paradigm was the fact that Javanese had not become the expression of an Indonesian identity. This would have awarded Java an intra-Indonesian dominance. Still, as we will see later on, Java retains a central and dominant position within Indonesia. Java bestowed this dominance to a larger extent on itself - driven by a healthy self confidence and the conviction of cultural supremacy. In its own recognition Java had always been more than just "primus inter pares."

Through the centuries the Javanese population accounted for 45 percent of the overall population of the archipelago. Add to this 14 percent Sundanese, who are populating the west of Java with their own language and culture. Java, consisting of the three provinces of *Java Barat* (Bandung), *Java Tengah* (Yogyakarta) and *Java Timur* (Surabaya), accounts for more than half of the

[22] Sukarno 1965, p.309. Emphasis in the original.
[23] See Ricklefs 1993², p.185.
[24] Gimonca Homepage w.o.y. 1910 to 1940.

Indonesian population.[25] In 1930 even 70 percent of the Indonesian population lived on the island of Java, which accounts for only seven percent of the land area of the archipelago. This was due to the extensive population growth, especially in Java, and the diminishing effect of the *transmigrasi* policy.[26] Against the background of this dominance it was only natural that a Javanese should become the impersonification of Indonesian nationalism: Sukarno.

Malay, which had been used as the lingua franca on the archipelago since centuries ago was the ideal linguistic hotbed for the idea of Indonesia. Additional help came from the fact that literature in Bahasa Indonesia did not have religion as a central topic; this supported the idea to build Indonesia as territorial national state and not as an islamic state which would exclude other religions (and hence other regions).[27]

It is important to point out that Indonesia is the only postcolonial state without a European language as the language of unity. One reason was that even the Dutch language was culturally too weak to embed itself as cultural and civilisational language across the islands. A second reason is that Indonesia, for a long time, until about 1830, was governed as a regional trading company. That Malay happened to become the self-evident language of the nationalists is a „curious accident".[28] This „curious accident" was

---

[25] Münch-Heubner 2000, p.34 and Ricklefs 1993², p.5.

[26] Ricklefs 1993², p.155 and p.165. Ricklefs also points to the immense population growth especially in Java and the failed repopulation programme *Transmigrasi*.

[27] See Ricklefs 1993², p.192.

[28] See Anderson 2003, p. 11 footnote 4 and p.110 footnote 62 and p.132.

helped by the fact that the *Partai Nasional Indonesia* (PNI), founded by Sukarno in 1927, declared promoting Bahasa Indonesia as the national language the cornerstone of their party program.[29]

Only after the end of the Javanese War in 1830 did the Dutch start to show real interest in a genuinely politically colonisation of the archipelago; this also marked the start of the actual colonial history of Java.[30] Diponegoro, the hero of the Javanese War, a rebellion against foreign occupation, became the role model for Sukarno. The Javanese War, just like the Padri War of the Minangkabau in West Sumatra under the leadership of Imam Tuanku Bonjol in the 1830s as well as other resistance movements, were only aiming at getting rid of the Dutch regime but were not aiming at independence of a unified *Indonesia Merdeka* (Free Indonesia).

The “new” nationalism was brought about by a new form of colonialism: the Dutch forced the Indonesians to cultivate products purely for export. This period became the most exploitative in the Indonesian colonial history.[31] By implementing the system of *cultuurstelsel*, or in Indonesian *Tanam Paksa* ("Enforcement Planting"), the Javanese were forced to cultivate products for export, mainly coffee, sugar and indigo, which hugely reduced the available acreage at the expense of daily staples, such as rice. Around 1845 famines afflicted Java, as poor harvests did not reap enough for the

---

[29] Schwarz 1999, p.4.

[30] Ricklefs 1993², p.119.

[31] Legge 2003³, p.45 and Ricklefs 1993², p.120.

population. This increased pressure on the colonial Dutch, as the local population deemed the *cultuurstelsel* unjust and unworthy. In 1860, the former Dutch colonial officer Eduard Douwes Dekker published the book *Max Havelaar* under the alias *Multatuli* and raised the awareness and consternation among the Dutch population back home. The discussion about a more liberal policy in Indonesia was started.[32] The alias *Multatuli* is Javanese for "I have suffered enough"; a name that spoke from the heart of many Javanese.[33] After 1870, in the hot phase of global colonialism, the pressure on the Dutch increased immensely to equally spread their influence and power over the whole archipelago. The Dutch were in danger of losing their territory to the other colonial powers of the region, especially the British, but also the Portuguese and Germans, and increasingly the US-Americans. Starting in 1900 the Dutch government in The Hague had to invest more into their colony than they were able to earn with the trade of raw materials.[34]

The year 1922 saw the establishment of the political definition of Indonesia. The *Perhimpunan Indonesia* (Indonesian Coalition, PI) were the first to use the name *Indonesia* as a political phrase indicating the unity of the archipelago.[35] The battle cry *Indonesia Merdeka* (Independent Indonesia) was supposed to help shed the name "Dutch-Indies" and establish an internationally recognised term while at the same time distancing itself from India and lend a linguistic face to the new *Vaterland*. It is worth knowing that

---

[32] See Gimonca Homepage w.o.y. 1830 to 1910 and Multatuli 1987 [1860].
[33] Winchester 2003, p.324.
[34] Gimonca Homepage w.o.y. 1830 to 1910.
[35] See Dahm 1966, p.40.

the term *merdeka* is Sanskrit for “rich” and was used in history to indicate real estate given away to monasteries; these in turn did not only grow rich, but also became socially independent.[36]

This is especially interesting against the background of the linguistic revolution. This revolution had introduced the Malay language, now Bahasa Indonesia, and was following the logic that the linguistic change was coherent with the abolishment of social- and status-related phrases and terms. The term Indonesia was coined by the German anthropologist Jordan who had studied the archipelago. Due to the proximity to India Jordan called the archipelago “the islands of the Indies”, in a syncrisis of the words *India* and the Greek word for island, *Nesos*, hence *Indusnesos*, which mutated over time into *Indonesia*.[37]

Under the strong influence of Sukarno the Indonesian notion gained followers as he considered it important that the concepts of a Greater Java or Greater Sumatra would be substituted by the idea of a Greater Indonesia.

In 1927 the term and notion of Indonesia were downright trending in Indonesian circles.[38] Critics however called the term Indonesia meaningless and empty as it would only derive meaning by relating to the Dutch-Indies.[39]

---

[36] See Dahm 1966, p.41, hier auch footnote 113.
[37] See Sukarno 1965, p.63.
[38] Dahm 1966, p.61.
[39] See Dahm 1966, p.69.

The goal of independence appeared strongly after 1926.[40] This was quite notable as, so Ricklefs, in 1905 there were neither an Indonesian unity nor common goals for which to fight. One of the main reasons was the fact that most political organisations, as well as the Muslim organisations, were at that time still organised along ethnic lines and hence emphasising intra-Indonesian differences and not commonalities.[41]

The time until 1927 however brought along several groundbreaking alterations. For one, Indonesia no longer defined itself as an ethnic state, but as geographic national state. By doing so, ethnic differences were abolished as a hurdle for national unity beyond the borders of an island. What is more, many colonial and administrative tasks were handed over to the Indonesians. As a corollary many Javanese, but also the Minangkabau of Sumatra, were taking on leadership functions. External influence had strongly and sustainably influenced Java and Sumatra and destroyed more of the prevalent old order. This in turn made the Javanese and the Minangkabau more receptive for new ideas. The Balinese or Acehnese were still fighting the initial colonial influence. Bali surrendered to the Dutch in 1906, after nearly all of the Balinese nobility died in the act of *puputan*, best described as an amok-like suicide, in this case by enemy fire. Aceh, depending on the point of view, has not accepted the central government to this day.[42] The Javanese and Minangkabau hence adopted a new identity much earlier. This led to a new social order and a reflection on the religious, social, political as

---

[40] See Dahm 1966, p.131 and Legge 2003[3], p.57.

[41] See Ricklefs 1993[2], p.57, p.147 and p.168.

[42] Gimonca Homepage w.o.y. 1830 to 1910.

well as economic circumstances. Against this background a new and genuinely Indonesian understanding began to grow.[43]

During the youth congress in 1928 in Batavia three ideals according to the motto *sumpah pemuda* were approved: one fatherland, Indonesia; one nation, Indonesia; one language, Bahasa Indonesia, the language of unity. The young people of Indonesia, who had gathered from all corners of the archipelago, wanted to show that they first and foremost regarded themselves as Indonesians.[44] Hence the year 1928 is commonly regarded as the actual starting point of Indonesian nationalism, as *kebangkitan bangsa*, national awakening.[45]

Also, in 1928 the *Partai Nasional Indonesia* (PNI) declared *merah-putih*, the red-white flag as the national flag and *Indonesia Raya* as national anthem. Both are still in use to this very day. These symbols helped establish the notion of Indonesia and expressed this in a political form. Sukarno, relating to the end of the islamic caliphate in 1924 and the growing communist movements around the globe, stated that "neither an airplane from Moscow nor a caliphate in Istanbul" would be able to free Indonesia - the struggle for independence was resting solely on the shoulder of the *pribumi*, the native people of Indonesia. Impressed by these developments and the necessity to spread the news over the whole archipelago, the first Indonesian news agency, *Antara*, started operating in 1937.[46]

---

[43] See Ricklefs 1993², p.163.
[44] See Ricklefs 1993², p.186.
[45] Gimonca Homepage w.o.y. 1910 to 1940.
[46] Gimonca Homepage w.o.y. 1910 to 1940. Translated.

In his negotiations with the Japanese during their occupation of the archipelago, Sukarno spoke about Indonesia, while the Japanese were relating mostly only to Java as administrative unit, as the rest of their occupied islands was organised in different administrational units. It is Sukarno's merit that Tokyo substituted Java with Indonesia during the occupation. The notion of a Greater Indonesia was now official and had moved onto the world stage. In the years to come most Southeast Asian nations would be gaining independence after 1945.[47]

Sukarno drew parallels to the archipelagos of Japan and Greece in his arguments for a united Indonesia. Sukarno argued that the Indonesian archipelago was a divinely ordained unity, just like the Japanese and Greek islands. In Indonesian history this had happened only twice before, once during the *Srivijaya* (7th-13th century) and *Majapahit* (13th-15th century) kingdoms.

Srivijaya was a hindu-buddhist seafaring nation whose inhabitants spoke an early form of Malay containing strong elements of Sanskrit. The power of the empire rested on trade relationships. Residence of the court was Palembang in Sumatra. After a revolt political refugees founded the kingdom of *Majapahit* in eastern Central Java. *Majapahit* stands out as one of the few examples successfully refuting the invasion of the Mongols when Kublai Khan tried to make landfall with an armada of 1,000 warships. The harbor and trading city *Malakka* was part of the *Majapahit* kingdom until 1511, when the Portuguese took over. *Majapahit* was the mightiest and most

[47] See Dahm 1966, p.210.

successful of all early-Javanese empires and was in no way inferior to *Angkor*. Hence the attractiveness for Sukarno.[48]

Now it was Sukarno's turn to lead the islands with god's will to a third union.[49] He even coined the term "geopolitics *Majapahit*."[50] Sukarno made ample use of the historic greatness of *Majapahit* in his argument for his new Indonesia:[51]

> *„The Majapahit Empire triumphed only after being tempered by hardship in the wars with Kublai Khan. Sultan Agung Hanjokrokoesoemo made the state of Mataram powerful after trials in the Senapti war. Not until the Crusades did Moslems in the golden age of Islam wax strong. Says God Almighty in the Koran: 'There are moments when your difficulties are useful and necessary!'"*[52]

In 1940, representatives of the Indonesian people, foremost Muhammad Thamrin, the chairman of the nationalist faction in the *Volksraad,* a representative body in which the Indonesians had been holding a majority since 1929, successfully introduced

[48] See Villiers 2000, p.93-118 and Gimonca Homepage w.o.y. Beginnings to 1500 and Friend 2003, p.8 and 19.
[49] See Dahm 1966, p.257.
[50] Dahm 1966, p.256.
[51] Friend 2003, p.19.
[52] Sukarno 1965, p.179.

a petition exchanging the term *Inlander* with *Indonesians* in all official documents.[53]

The Second World War and the occupation by the Japanese were an important step into the direction of independence from the Dutch. This might sound paradoxical as the Japanese terror regime was the worst the Indonesian people had to suffer.[54]

The Japanese outlawed all nationalist organisations, the red-white flag and also abolished the *Volksraad,* the representative body which the Indonesians had used to proclaim their policies. But the Japanese also detained all Dutch citizens. This created a huge vacuum in local administration and other parts of society, and the Japanese filled this vacuum with Indonesians. The same was true for the churches: incarcerated Dutch priests had left their converted congregations unattended. These posts were now filled in by Indonesians.

Indonesian Muslims however had quite a different problem with the Japanese: all subdued Indonesians now had to take a bow in the direction of the Japanese emperor in Tokyo - depending on the occasion, several times a day. Their religion prohibited those bows, as Muslims were only allowed to bow towards Mecca. This duty-to-bow towards Tokyo was finally abolished by the Japanese, at least for the majority Muslim part of the population.

In July 1942 Sukarno accepted the appointment as Indonesian head of government, reporting directly to the Japanese military.

---

53 See Ricklefs 1993², p.194 and Gimonca Homepage w.o.y. 1910 to 1940.
54 Schwarz 1999, p.5.

One year before their surrender, the Japanese issued the first *Rupiah* bill, with the Indonesian language imprinted on it. By creating a vision for the geographical form of Indonesia, most influential Indonesians voted for unifying all peoples of Malay origin under the umbrella of the new Indonesia. This of course included the British colonial territories of Malaysia and in the final instance lead to Sukarno's policy of *Konfrontasi* during the 1960s and Indonesia's subsequent war against Malaysia.[55]

In addition to bringing political awareness and activity to the Indonesian people by increasing their participation in the administration[56], the Japanese period was a period of emphasising the dominance of Java within the archipelago. What is more, the Japanese had equipped Sukarno and his deputy, Hatta, after their stringent urging, with a political organisation that would render it far easier for the two to entice and mobilise the masses later on.

As we will see, the Indonesian military has its roots in a homeland defence corps that was actually introduced by the Japanese. But the biggest gift the Japanese made to the Indonesians was their defeat in the Second World War. This produced, only two days after Tokyo's capitulation, on 17 August 1945, the ideal historic moment for Sukarno and Muhammad Hatta to proclaim *Indonesia Merdeka.* The power vacuum in Batavia helped Sukarno to get the upper hand. This was urgent for Indonesia as Burma and the Philippines had been granted a puppet government in 1943. And the "(...) the Japanese

---

[55] Gimonca Homepage w.o.y. 1940 to 1945.
[56] See hierzu auch Schwarz 1999, p.11.

(...) were losing control of the popular forces they were unleashing." This ended with a half-hearted promise to grant Indonesia statehood at an undefined point of time in the future.[57]

The first Indonesian standing army, consisting of volunteers, was founded in 1943 and had the name of *Pembela Tanah Air* (PETA), the protectors of the fatherland. PETA forged the leading fighters for Indonesia's independence, foremost the later general Sudirman.[58] By the middle of 1945 PETA counted 120,000 armed fighters. On 5 October 1945 PETA was renamed *Tentara Nasional Indonesia* (TNI), the official armed forces of Indonesia, a term still in use today.[59] After Indonesian forces had occupied the postal-, telegraph- and telephone offices, the government issued the first stamps; most of the stamps however were Japanese, with the text *Repoeblik Indonesia* printed over the Japanese symbols. In 1947 Indonesians for the first time issued their own *Rupiah* billp.[60]

The Indonesian national state is not a product of western colonialism, as the Dutch, in contrast to other colonial powers in Africa or Indochina, were not separating or throwing together endemic ethnicities by artificial boundaries. After their withdrawal they largely left intact the old system of states, just as they had found them upon their first arrival. The system of indirectly trying to govern through contracts or trade deals had attempted to influence the existing powers and to play with their

---

[57] Ricklefs 1993², p.199 and p.203, p.207.

[58] See Ricklefs 1993², p.206.

[59] Gimonca Homepage w.o.y. 1940 to 1945.

[60] Gimonca Homepage w.o.y. 1945 to 1950.

balance.[61] Even the very short-lived British intermezzo in Indonesia during the early 19th century, while Napoleon occupied the Netherlands, did not change this.[62]

The idea of a unified Indonesia is the central topic of every acting president.[63] The Indonesian national motto, derived from the Sanskrit, focuses on diversity: *Bhinekka Tunggal Ika,* which can be translated as *E Pluribus Unum*,[64] or, far more appropriate, "Different but One", or more streamlined, "All is One".[65] This is the deepest cognition of Javanese philosophy and was Sukarno's nation-building notion. Sukarno was the one out of many who melded all into one and thus founded Indonesia.

Let's have a closer look at the very cornerstones of Sukarno's political philosophy.

---

[61] See Münch-Heubner 2000, p.10.
[62] See z.B. Barley 2002.
[63] Schwarz 1999, p.6.
[64] Friend 2003, p.9.
[65] See Dahm 1966, p.264f.

The cornerstones of Indonesian nationalism

To understand the political origin of Indonesia we must first comprehend several decisively important Javanese phrases.

Gotong-royong

Gotong-Royong is "the voluntary and mutual help that is being offered in Java as in many other parts" of Indonesia for all kinds of tasks.[66] Sukarno made use of *gotong-royong* especially to distinguish the generally oriental and specifically Indonesian concept of equality of all (especially in the fight for independence) from the occidental and western concepts of individualism and liberalism. By doing so the newly born Indonesian society should always take precedence over individuals.

More specifically this principle should emphasise the unity between rich and poor, the believers of different faiths as well as between locals and foreigners. *Gotong-royong* peaked politically in 1960, when a *gotong-royong*-parliament was called to life.[67]

---

[66] Dahm 1966, p.155.

[67] See Dahm 1966, p.155f, p.219, p.263 and p.266 and Ricklefs 1993^2, p.255.

Gotong-royong represents a genuinely Indonesian condition and hence correlates deeply to the Indonesian soul. *Gotong-royong* is the term to which the Indonesia of Sukarno can be reduced to.[68]

---

[68] Legge 2003[3], p.322.

Ratu-adil

Bernhard Dahm, in the introductory chapter of his book, shows us the importance of Javanese mythology for the Indonesian battle for independence. In this context, the term *Ratu-Adil* has a special meaning.[69] *Ratu-Adil* actually means "messiah" or "just king." The arrival of a *Ratu-Adil* was actually prophesied to the Javanese by *Djajabaja* and should bring the happening of all imaginable good, from freedom from taxes to houses built of stone and coincide with the termination of foreign rule. *Djajabaja* was a descendant from the *walis*, the holies of Mecca. The different names of the certificate of descent of the *Ratu-Adil*, *Si Tandjung Putih* or *Erutjakra*, are an example of the syncretism of Java, which combines hindu, buddhist and islamic ideas in the figure of the *Djajabaja* as well as the *Ratu-Adil.* The mythological birth date of *Djajabaja* happened to be the middle of the 18th century when the Dutch were violently separating the Javanese kingdom *Mataram*[70]: only under the leadership of an influential spiritual being could the yoke of the occupiers be discarded.

The name *Djajabaja* has its origins in the 12th century, when the king of Kediri, *Jaya Bhaya,* ordered the translation of the Indian *Mahabharata* into the Javanese and made the battle of the *Pendawas* against the *Kaurawas* well-known and popular.[71]

---

[69] See Dahm 1966, p.1-15.

[70] Villiers 2000, p.286-288. Ricklefs, 1993^2, p.109-114.

[71] See below.

The prophecy of the arrival of the *Ratu-Adil* from abroad came to life with the arrival of Sir Stamford Raffles in 1811. Raffles was supposed to hand back Java to the Javanese and expel the other foreigners, the Dutch, from the island. Only the Japanese however were seen as incarnation of the *Ratu-Adil* as they were in fact expelling the Dutch from Java (or, to be correct, detaining them). The legend of the *Djajabaja* prophesied the arrival of "small yellow humans from the north." The Japanese were the perfect cast for this role and played their part very well.[72] Meanwhile Diponegoro, the aforementioned hero of the Javanese war from 1825 to 1830, brought himself up for the role as he started calling himself by the name of *Erutjakra*.[73] In addition, Javanese mythology interpreted the auguries of nature to be able to forecast the arrival of the *Ratu-Adil*. The *Ratu-Adil*-exclamation in Cilegon in 1888, the farmers' revolt in Banten in the same year, both in West-Java, directly referred to the tremendous explosion of the volcano Krakatoa on 27 August 1883 in the Street of Sanda.[74] *Cokroaminoto*, the leader of *Sarekat Islam*, the most influential nationalist Indonesian union of that time, hijacked the explosion of Krakatoa for his personal fame by trying to connect his birth in 1882 to this natural disaster. Was *Cokroaminoto* the new *Ratu-Adil*? Depending on how it was written[75] the name *Cakra-aminata*, i.e. *Cokroaminoto*, contained a part of the name *Eru-cakra*.[76] *Sarekat Islam* became the greatest *Ratu-Adil*-movement in the history of

[72] See Dahm 1966, p.164f. Friend 2003, p.88.
[73] See Dahm 1966, p.1-6.
[74] See Dahm 1966, p.6f and Winchester 2003, p.317-338.
[75] In 1972 Indonesia and Malaysia conducted a spelling reform. Hence dj became j; j became y; tj became c; and oe became a u. Schwarz 1999, p.448.
[76] See Ricklefs 1993[2], p.167.

the archipelago. *Cokroaminoto* later explained that socialism was the *Ratu-Adil* Indonesia was actually looking for. With this statement *Sarekat Islam* said goodbye to the mythological figure of *Ratu-Adil*. This gave way for Sukarno to transform the *Ratu-Adil* into the authoritarian savior whose rule would end in chaos.[77]

The influence and impact of *Ratu-Adil* should not be underestimated in the history of the Indonesian nationalism:

"These developments (around Ratu-Adil*) exacerbated the xenophobic character that was inherent in the prophecies of* Djajabaja *and helped create the readiness among the rural population for nationalistic ideas."*[78]

The *Ratu-Adil* also defended the Javanese order, the *Tata,* against intruders from the outside.

[77] See Dahm 1966, p.12f, p.15 and p.28 and Friend 2003, p.49f and p.255.
[78] Dahm 1966, p.7.

Tata

The *Ratu-Adil* takes center stage in the Javanese mythology as he is the defender of *Tata*, "the well-ordered harmony of Javanese Weltanschauung."[79] For Sukarno, the Dutch were the foreign invaders disturbing the *Tata*. Javanese syncretism has its roots in the *Tata* as it absorbed all external elements as long as they were not disturbing the order. In case of a violation the Javanese duty calls for the execution of *wahju tjakraningrat*: the mandate of ensuring the *Tata*. Sukarno felt that he was the executioner of this mandate. Sukarno's seemingly endless willingness to compromise on the inside and absolute unwillingness to compromise on the outside stems from the *Tata*. In the political history of Indonesia the difference between the Javanese philosophy and those of other islands, foremost Sumatra, became apparent in the fact that Sukarno's strongest antagonists who neither shared his ideology or Weltanschauung came from Sumatra: Sjahrir, Hatta, Natsir and Salim.[80]

The concept of *Mufakat* made sure that the other islands' viewpoints found consideration during the nation building process.

---

[79] Dahm 1966, p.264.
[80] See Dahm 1966, p.152 and p.264.

Permusyawaratan and mufakat

Permusyawaratan is a precondition for *mufakat. Mufakat* actually means to agree, to consent. The Javanese cosmos regards all to be one, and decisions have been taken in a way that all partners can consent and are not marginalised by decisions of a majority (this contradicts, obviously, the western notion of a representative democracy in which the majority decides). To be able to actually achieve that state of common positive agreement, an overall discussion, or *permusyawaratan*, needs to take place during which all contrasting opinions are compromised to the extent that all partners can achieve the *mufakat.*

Sukarno explained that the western concept of majority equalled a tyranny of the majority over the minority. Hence the parliamentary system, as introduced by the Sumatran Sutan Sjahrir, the first prime minister of the republic, failed early on. Obviously the biggest disadvantage of the system is the inability to derive at clear decisions as all opinions need to be respected. For Sukarno this was the Indonesian way of democracy, and for the minorities the guarantee that their voices would be heard. This right to codetermination, similar to *Wayang*, had a huge influence on the unity of the multi-ethnic archipelago.[81]

[81] See Dahm 1966, p.62f, p. 98, p.154, p.256.

Wayang

The *Wayang* is a shadowplay with leather puppets being directed with a stick from below and their movements are projected onto a drape. The *Dalang* narrates stories from the Javanese mythology, usually from dusk till dawn.[82] The function of *Wayang* is to find ideals in the characters and the realisation of personal dreams. The *Ramayana* and the *Mahabharata* are the basis of many Javanese stories and a means of communication between the Javanese.[83] Sukarno explains this in his biography:

> *„I'm a master at choosing words so foreigners who speak the language cannot catch the regional idiom. I'd play on* Mahabharata *stories because 80 percent of all Indonesians were weaned on them. They know Ardjuna is the hero of five brothers whose kingdoms were falsely taken in a great war. Those five represent good. The invaders represent evil."*[84]

From the *Ramayana* derived the *Hikayat Seri Rama*, and from the *Mahabharata* the *Hikayat Pandawa Jaya*, as well as the

[82] See Friend 2003, p.88.
[83] See Dahm 1966, p.17-19 and Friend 2003, p.88 and p.264.
[84] Sukarno 1965, p.179.

Bharatayuddha, containing the deepest secrets and characters of Java:

> *„It [the wayang] featured figures with Javanised names, evolved local characteristics, and innovated characters who acted in a world of arcane allusions and tantalising prophecies. Predictions were capable of being denied as never meant, or as misunderstood if they fail to come to pass, and equally capable, in retrospect, of being averred as clearly foreseen, had one only heard aright and remembered the metaphorical bounty offered by whatever prophet or guru was speaking."*[85]

The hindu core of the stories survived the islamisation of Java; Ricklefs even discerns the "task" of the *Wayang* to safeguard the hindu-buddhist inheritance on the island of Java, or even more so to protect the memory of the hindu-buddhist origins.[86]

The *Mahabharata* depicts the battle between the *Pendawas* and the *Kaurawas* about the kingdom of *Ngastina* which rightly belongs to the *Pendawas* but is currently occupied by the *Kaurawap.* This play is therefore a nationalist's bonanza of paradigms mirroring the idea of an occupied Indonesia:

---

[85] Friend 2003, p.260.

[86] See Ricklefs 1993[2], p.52f and p.164. Legge 2003[3], p.32.

"That villagers could understand Sukarno in terms of wayang *models merely reflects the subtlety and richness of that art form and Sukarno's own love of* wayang *and skill in the manipulation of symbols. "*[87]

The fight of the protagonist, the *Bharata-Judah,* was to become the battle of Sukarno on the side of the *Pendawas.*

The Javanese Weltanschauung does not know the simple black-and-white view. Java resembled a microcosm within a macrocosm, in which the good as well as the evil had their rights to exist. This view was only able to be maintained while no other outsiders were invading this Javanese order. Only with the idea of the *Ratu-Adil* and the occupational power in form of the Europeans who, unlike Hinduism, Buddhism and Islam would not fit into the *Tata,* did the concept of either-or win in influence. [88]

The influence of the *Wayang* was still visible in the middle of the 20th century in Indonesian politics as the Japaneses made use of the *Wayang* to spread their message.[89] During the phase of the „Guided Democracy" (1957-65) Sukarno was the *Dalang*, the puppets master and the power hub. The good always has its place to the right of the *Dalang*, while the bad has to sit to the left. In 1965 with coup and counter coup ousting Sukarno from power,

---

[87] Ricklefs 1993², p.258.
[88] See Dahm 1966, p.17-19 and Friend 2003, p.88 and p.264.
[89] Ricklefs 1993², p.202.

the opponents of the communists (and finally of Sukarno) knew: the PKI (*Partai Komunis Indonesia*) was way too far to the left of Sukarno and hence the *mufakat* no longer possible.[90]

Sukarno grew up as a child watching *Wayang* plays. His fascination for the *Wayang* did not wane during his lifetime.[91] Sukarno writes about his incarceration in the Bantjeuj prison from 1929-31:

> *"Shouting the Wayang not only entertained and relaxed me, it comforted and strengthened me. The dark shadows in my thought melted away as mist and I was able to sleep with this reaffirmation of my faith that good will triumph over evil."*[92]

---

[90] See Sukarno 1965, p.179 and Legge 2003³, p.448.
[91] Dahm 1966, p.17ff.
[92] Sukarno 1965, p.102.

Sukarno, the father of Indonesian nationalism

“I have made myself the meeting place of all trends and ideologies. I have blended, blended, and blended them until finally they became the present Sukarno.”[93] Sukarno has not only managed to unify the different Javanese concepts in himself but also, as a Javanese, to combine nationalism, socialism and islam.

Sukarno, the Javanese

To understand Sukarno we need to grasp Javanese culture as a whole. The following metaphor can help:

> *„Javanese culture is like a tapeworm. It is very unlike the tooth and claw of the Russian bear, or the Chinese dragon, or the lion of the Netherlands or the UK, or the beak and talon of the American eagle. It is ‘aesthetic’ and silent; it is polite (no commotion); it is insinuating. It weakens without turmoil and it is ultimately deadly. Javanese culture, like the*

[93] Sukarno, quoted in Schwarz 1999, p.1.

tapeworm, cannot be yanked out or cut out. It will require strong and repeated doses of medicine to 'free it out.'"[94]

The Javanese culture is rather introvert. The tensions between the orthodox Muslims, the *Santri*, and the only by name faithful, the *Abangan*, play an important role as the latter represent a very modern face of Islam containing many non-islamic features, mainly derived from Hinduism or Buddhism.

We also need to keep in mind the difference of islamic law and the *adat*, the „custom law“. The Javanese syncretism represents an extreme difference to the rest of the archipelago and led (and still leads) to strife between the different islands. The very fact that the Javanese population accounts for more than half of the overall population does not help. Also, the level of Dutch penetration was highest in Java.[95]

Sukarno, as incarnation of Javanese culture, radiated an immense self confidence and "in the eyes of the masses he equalled the nimbus of the chosen, the *Ratu-Adil.*“[96] This went too far for Mohammad Hatta. He publicly criticised the deification by Sukarno's disciples.[97] Sukarno however never tried to take advantage of the superstition of his people; he followed Cokroaminoto by declaring the *Ratu-Adil* to be independence, participation in government or socialism.[98] He was helped by

[94] Mangunwijaya, Y.B., quoted in Friend 2003, p.259.

[95] Legge 2003^3, p.58f and Ricklefs 1993^2, p.154.

[96] Dahm 1966, p.263.

[97] See Dahm 1966, p.129.

[98] Dahm 1966, p.94.

choosing as his ideal in the *Wayang* the figure of *Bima* who, as one of the five adamant heros in the *Mahabharata,* was impersonating the fear of the enemy until they, the *Kaurawas*, were beaten. *Bima's* and Sukarno's main trait were the same: the sentimental readiness to compromise internally, and the grim unwillingness to compromise with the enemy.
And Sukarno's enemy was always the same: the West, whether as individualism, liberalism, in form of the Dutch or the US-Americans.

Sukarno's father, under the influence of the *Wayang,* changed his son's name from *Kusno* in Sukarno. Sukarno is derived from *Karno,* a famous *Ksatrija,* a fighter in the *Mahabharata,* whose courage and honesty were without equal. Sukarno often compared himself to *Kokrosono,* another figure in the *Wayang*, brandishing a wonder weapon, the *Nanggala,* which he used, as rhetoric power, to bring back people who had misunderstood him in the first place.[99] Of course Sukarno not only made use of these aforementioned figures but dug deep into his rich knowledge of the *Wayang* to stay at the peak of power.[100] This also involved mentioning the negative traits of Javanese culture which Sukarno utilised to drive forward *Indonesia Merdeka*.

> *"Power tends to corrupt, and the closer to power a Javanese is, the worst of his culture comes out . . . The Javanese way of communication is broaching things*

[99] See Dahm 1966, p.20, p.103 and p.263 sowie Legge 2003³, p.33.
[100] Siehe dazu: Friend 2003, p.88. Sukarno does not mention *Bima* in his autobiography. Instead *Gatotkaca*, a fighter for the good, is his hero.

away from the edge of, from the view of power. There is no concept of conflict management . . . Even agreements imply power relations. And if you are really strong, you are free to do what you wish to do. You don't need *agreement. [...] Javanese cannot distinguish between communication and manipulation."*[101]

Even though Sukarno applied the Javanese syncretism to his political goals, he never managed to get the same level of fondness and sympathy from the non-Javanese part of the population. Sukarno was the founder of his own form of Indonesian nationalism but he always stayed true to his Javanese roots and failed to be a „uniter of all“. In literature, Legge agrees with Dahm: Sukarno can only be understood properly within the context of the Javanese culture. His *mufakat*-attitude was only the most superficial of all Javanese traits.

Sukarno needs to be understood as charismatic leader in the sense of Max Weber and to the same degree as person yielding extraordinary authority. His rhetoric swayed the masses and made him the „Lion of the Podium“[102], and he lived up to his promises of really being the leader of his people. This had self-reinforcing effects and he was able to utilise all social levels as power base in Java and Sanda. They in turn were ascribing him supernatural powers. This power, the *kesaktian* enabled him as *Ratu-Adil* to restore the balancing harmony between the

[101] Magnis-Suseno, Franz, quoted in Friend 2003, p.495f.
[102] Legge 2003[3], p.105.

worldly order and the cosmos. His use of traditional symbols and later, of his presidential palace, transformed Sukarno into a modern Hindu-Javanese king.

The assumption that Sukarno had supernatural powers lend his love life a special focus. His ample use of *Wayang* in his rhetoric made him more easily understood by the Javanese and Sundanese than by followers from other islands; in times of strict censure by the Dutch this was important for Sukarno:[103]:

> *"Was this simply a matter of rhetorical skill? [...] Or did he himself move in the thought world of the* wayang*? There are many signs that he did tend to think of the events of the day as illustrating* wayang *themes [...]. Such a frame of reference gave an heroic character to his struggle, but it may also explain his occasional miscalculations of the power realities of a situation and his tendency almost to expect miraculous solutions."* [104]

In reality, Sukarno never was anything less than the master puppet player, the *Dalang.* He was the only one to run the country.[105]

---

[103] Legge 2003³, p.19-22, p.204 and p.348f.
[104] Legge 2003³, p.22.
[105] Legge 2003³, p.400.

Sukarno, the nationalist

Sukarno is a product of his time. The post-colonial era brought forward charismatic leaders in Africa and Asia: Gandhi and Nehru, Mao, before that Sun Yat-sen and Ho Chi Minh. In this context Sukarno can be seen as a typical nationalist figure. Sukarno converted the islamic form of head-cover, the *Pitji,* into the uniform of Indonesian nationalism: "We need a symbol of the Indonesian personality. This individualised cap, synonymous with the common worker of the Malay race, is indigenous to our people. The name even devolved from our conquerors. The Dutch word 'pet' means cap. 'Je' being the diminutive implying 'little', the word is actually 'petje'. I say, let us hold our heads high bearing this cap as a symbol of Free Indonesia."[106] The difference to the afore-mentioned leaders rests in the details of how Sukarno was coining his own ideology: his form of Indonesian nationalism. This ideological approach clearly elevates Sukarno over the others.[107]

In 1926, at the age of 25, Sukarno started preaching nationalism. The demands on him were that intense that he had to shut down his engineering business.[108] In Sukarno's eyes nationalism was "as wide as air" and hence was the vehicle to unify all anti-imperialist, anti-western groups from all over Asia.[109]

---

[106] Sukarno 1965, p.51f.

[107] Legge 2003[3], p.15f, p.105 and p.380ff.

[108] Sukarno 1965, p.72.

[109] See Dahm 1966, p.53.

His central political question after independence was how to *best* build an Indonesian nation against the background of all the differences.[110] Sukarno's nationalism was the common denominator of all groups during the fight for independence.[111] Sukarno declared his view of Indonesian nationalism during the Japanese occupation:

> *"Real nationalists, who found their love for their fatherland on the knowledge of the structure of the global economy and history and not only on national hubris, nationalists, who are chauvinists, not only can, but have to refute all parochial ideas of exclusiveness. Real nationalists, whose nationalism is not only a copy of western nationalism, but a nationalism resting on a feeling of love towards humans and humankind, nationalists whose feeling of nationalism is godly inspiration (*wahju*) and whose realisation is a service to god (*bakti*) are free from all imaginations of pettiness and limitedness. For them their love towards their (own) nation is great and wide and also has space for other thoughts, just like air is big and wide and*

[110] Legge 2003³, p.373.
[111] See Dahm 1966, p.51ff.

offers space to all who need them to live."[112]

While delivering a speech on radio Sukarno criticised the pettiness and narrow mindedness of his co-fighters - especially Sjahrir, Hatta and Natsir. According to Sukarno, they were thinking "in centimeters" and were focusing on petty details instead of inflaming the nationalist spirit.[113] Sukarno radiated a sympathy that made the masses love him and that turned him into a nationalist philanthropist:

> *"The love for my fatherland is part of my love for all humankind. I am a patriot because I am a human being and humane. Nobody is excluded from my love."*[114]

This attitude was crucial for Sukarno's success, as orthodox Muslims and the ethnic Chinese were strongly opposed against Indonesian nationalism. His nationalist synthesis tried to define Indonesian multi-ethnicity against the West. According to the *mufakat* national unity was worth any pricc.[115]

The Dutch school system needs to be mentioned in this context. Under Snouck Hurgronje, during the time of the Ethnic Policy, a liberal policy in Dutch politics founded on humanistic ideas, the

[112] Sukarno, in Dahm 1966, p.52.
[113] Dahm 1966, p.262.
[114] Sukarno, quoting Gandhi, in Dahm 1966, p.52.
[115] See Dahm 1966, p.119, p.257 and p.263.

Dutch educated local Indonesians, just like Sukarno, in a western manner. The Dutch however failed to offer those academics adequate jobs, meaning they created an elite without purpose who, in their unhappiness, fell back into their own society.

> *"Western education had alienated some intellectuals from their own society and its preconceptions, making them sons of the Enlightenment, but without making them Europeans."*[116]

The *Volksraad,* established in 1918, did not change anything as Indonesians were not given any real influence.

To fully understand the impact of the western educational system we have to contrast it with the prevalent Indonesian one, as it dominated Javanese schools in 1922. The *Taman Siswa* refuted Islam on the one hand, but focused on Javanese culture on the other. Education included the unique synthesis of Hinduism, Buddhism, Islam as well as western concepts.[117] And it made use of the Javanese concept of self help, *Gotong-Royong.*[118] It is clear that especially Sukarno assumed this schooling system to be ideal for Indonesia.

As the illiteracy quote was very high, it became clear that masses were influenced by the educated Indonesians. Their message was: Dutch occupation is unjust and unjustified. The new

---

[116] Legge 2003[3], p.53.
[117] Ricklefs 1993[2], p.182.
[118] See Hatta 1957, p.8.

intelligentsia streamlined the dissatisfaction and Sukarno turned it into a political power. "Together with the Dutch" turned into "without the Dutch." The idea of unity in form of a nation gave Sukarno a new reason to exist.[119]

In addition, the Japanese made use of the educated Indonesians after most of the Dutch had been interned. Sukarno was awarded the highest honor when the Tenno himself shook hands only with him during a visit in 1943.[120]

Sukarno's nationalism married the idea of the state to the idea of socialism. This "eastern" is different from the "western" nationalism by turning its supporters into "tools of god" and leading towards a "spiritual life", thereby focusing the idea of nationalism on the inside and not on an aggressiveness against the outside world.[121]

---

[119] See Legge 2003[3], p.50ff and Dahm 1966, p.8ff. Anderson 2003, p.121ff. Ricklefs 1993[2], p.151ff.

[120] Dahm 1966, p.119, p.195.

[121] Dahm 1966, p.119, p.135.

Sukarno, father of the marhaen

In his autobiography Sukarno is dedicating a whole chapter to *Marhaenism*.[122] At the age of 20, Sukarno decided one morning to skip class at the university of Bandung. On this morning a unique and important concept for the future of Indonesia was born. The young Sukarno asked a farmer on his rice paddy whether the tools he was using also belonged to him. With his beggarly possessions and a hand-to-mouth life this farmer represented the sheer infinite number of Javanese farmers with a similar fate. The name of this farmer was a common name in Java: *Marhaen*. From now on the *Marhaen* were Sukarno's symbol for the future people of Indonesia, who were mostly farmers:

> *"Our farmers till infinitesimal patches of soil. They are end products of the feudal system under which the first peasant was exploited by the first feudal lord and on down through the centuries. Even those of us who are not farmers are victims of the Dutch trade imperialism, victims whose ancestors were forced into minimal enterprises to eke out an existence. These who constitute nearly*

[122] Sukarno 1965, p.61-68.

the whole Indonesian population are Marhaenists.*"*[123]

Since this day, Sukarno has been using the phrase *Marhaenism* as his symbol for national identity. He defined the phrase with "Indonesian Socialism in operation", and the *Marhaen* as „a little man with little ownership, little tools, sufficient to himself."[124]

Sukarno's philanthropy, loving humans and humankind, has its roots in the farmer *Marhaen*, who opened Sukarno's heart for the poor people.[125] This at least is the official version. But, according to Legge, it is also possible that the ever-scheming Sukarno invented *Marhaen* to simply gain political success of this story. The concept of *Marhaenism* rests on the poverty of a huge part of the population and hence can bridge the gaps between the different islands, religions, ethnicities as well as occupations, that is the farmer, the street vendor, without having to be more precise or to show more content for itself. Hence he addressed this concept to all Indonesians who were supposed to refute the capitalism of their own people. This unifying effect is the specific Indonesian idiosyncrasy of *Marhaenism*,[126] and hence we can call it a "*Marhaenist* nationalism, socio-nationalism or socio-democracy": freedom knows no classes and the fight for it is international.[127]

---

[123] Sukarno 1965, p.62.

[124] Sukarno 1965, p.63.

[125] Friend 2003, p.26.

[126] See Legge 2003[3], p.86 and p.385 and Dahm 1966, p.114.

[127] Dahm 1966, p.111, p.113f and p.119. Dahm offers a wonderful explanation of Sukarno's Marxist analysis of Western capitalism. Ibid., p.109-121.

In addition to being a moderate socialist, Sukarno also was a *Haji*, a Muslim who had made the pilgrimage to Mecca. Being a Javanese, Sukarno saw no contradiction in being a socio-nationalist and a Muslim at the same time.

Sukarno, the Muslim

Sukarno's god, the one he worshiped, was not the purely islamic god who demanded an absolute submission to his commandments, but it was "the god of fate, justified by the developments of global affairs, whose inspiration you received and interpreted at your own discretion." For Sukarno, the Javanese Muslim, or better, the Muslim Javanese, god was the "big unity."[128]

Sukarno's spiritual part is preceded by an interesting development in Indonesia. On the one hand, since 1909 *Sarekat Dagang Islamiyah* (SDI) had managed to represent the interests of islam as well as the traders. In 1912 the SDI changed their name as well as program: she was now the *Sarekat Islam* (SI), the Islamic Union, connecting Muslims between Java and the rest of the archipelago. Under the leadership of Cokroaminoto she gained immense influence; Cokroaminoto as well as the SI in turn held considerable sway over Sukarno.[129]

At the same time, starting in Cairo, the school of *Modernism* gained influence in Indonesian islam, and laid the foundation of a new era. The Modernism mainly argued for a reform in education and for an integration of western concepts into islam.[130] The Minangkabau played a central part in this, as their

---

[128] Dahm 1966, p.260.
[129] See Ricklefs 1993², p.166-168.
[130] Barton 2002, p.12f.

newspaper *al Imam* was read by a majority of the population. Most of the Indonesians were (and are) Sunnis and followers of the school of *Shafi'i*. Especially in Java, but not only there, Sufism was (and is) very present. In 1912 the largest and to this day most influential modern islamic union was founded in Yogyakarta: *Muhammadiyah* (Followers of Muhammad).[131]

Following these developments, a number of interesting concepts appeared: Haji Agus Salim, a Minangkabau, openly spoke in 1917 in front of SI to combine Modernism and Pan-Islamism as basis for all political activity. Yet another haji, Haji Misbach, also known as the "Red Haji", claimed that islam and communism were the same: out of this train of thought was born, in 1924, the PKI, the *Partai Komunis Indonesia*. Haji Misbach followed the vision of the rebirth of the old *Majapahit*, where a society without classes was realised.[132] Modernism as nationalist basis however failed as the Javanese were not relying on islam strongly enough.

Nearly at the same time, in 1926, the orthodox Muslims of Indonesia united themselves in the *Nahdlatul Ulama* (NU), which means as much as "The awakening of the religious scholar".[133]

---

[131] See Ricklefs 1993², p.171 and Schwarz 1999, p.4.

[132] See Ricklefs 1993², p.173f.

[133] Barton 2002, p.13 and Ricklefs 1993², p.177. NU today has more than 40 million followers and is the largest Muslim community in the world. Before becoming President Abdurrahman Wahid was the chairperson. Barton 2002.

Islam continued to lose political clout as the religion was mainly leaning on ethnic-based organisations and hence never represented a concept for all of Indonesia. For the political leaders, national unity and independence were more important than islam - in contrast, the *Muhammadiyah* as well as the NU wanted to achieve an islamic state. The most radical islamic movements detested nationalist ideas as they wanted to erect an islamic theocracy. Several Minangkabau, who had studied in Cairo and had seen the failure of the caliphate of Istanbul, were convinced that an Indonesian islamic theocracy would fail and hence brought home the idea of uniting the concepts of islam and nationalism. Cokroaminoto became on of the most prominent representatives of pan-islamism; this development presented the the definite ideological separation between him and Sukarno.[134]
The umbrella organisation *Masyumi* - before Sukarno abolished it - was a vehicle for some Muslims to formulate one goal: the demand for a theocracy and the opinion, that the *Pancasila* is undermining the influence of islam in Indonesia.[135] Sukarno was influenced by all of the above. His Javanese "all is one" helped him create the synthesis of nationalism, socialism and islam and lend it its "three-dimensional maturity."[136]

This synthesis is the "actual key for understanding" Sukarno.[137]
In combination with his interpretation that nationalism was "as wide as air" he urged for a close cooperation with islam: "All

---

[134] See Ricklefs 1993², p.179f and p.184 and p.190.
[135] Schwarz 1999, p.9.
[136] Sukarno 1965, p.74.
[137] Dahm 1966, p.33.

Indonesian groups need to be united, need to be one, to be able to achieve freedom."[138]

Sukarno studied islam intensively. During his exile in Flores and Benkulu in Sumatra, from 1934 to 1941 he immersed himself in the koran and developed his own idea and interpretation of the religion:[139]

> *"Let's not focus on each letter. Let's focus on the spirit, the soul of the letter. Only in this way can we free islam from the contradictions of the letters and hence from the casuistic of the Fakhists. Only in this way can we think independently, act independently, and study independently - guided only by a compass: the spirit of the (real) islam."* [140]

Only this free interpretation of islam made it possible that Sukarno denied islam to be part of the official principle of governing in Indonesia, the *Pancasila*.

---

[138] Dahm 1966, p.54 and p.80.

[139] A complete overview of Sukarno and islam, see Dahm 1966, p.133-150.

[140] Sukarno, quoted in Dahm 1966, p.147.

Sukarno and the Pancasila

Before we look at the Pancasila in details, let us recap the basis on which Sukarno built this concept. The foundation is Indonesian socialism, different to other forms of socialism as it is not a purely materialistic concept: Indonesia, after all, is "god's own country." Sukarno introduced political equality in form of the American Declaration of Independence, spiritual equality with islam and christianity and scientific equality with Marx. „To this mixture we add the National identity: *Marhaenism*. Then we sprinkle in *Gotong Royong* [...]. Mix it all up and the result is Indonesian Socialism."[141]

As we already know, Sukarno himself is the result of Javanism, mysticism, theosophy in form of islam, hinduism, buddhism, humanism, socialism and nationalism. Intellectually he added Marx and Jefferson, Sun Yat-sen and Gandhi. This is the light in which Sukarno wants to be seen and understood. „What came out has been called – in plain terms – Sukarnoism."[142] This mixture does not fall "into a box according to the Western mind but, then, you must remember I do not have a Western mind. [...] I fit into no pattern politically, which is, perhaps, why I am subject to so much misunderstanding."[143] Against this background we now undertake to understand the *Pancasila*, Indonesia's philosophy of state.

141 Sukarno 1965, p.75.
142 Sukarno 1965, p.76.
143 Sukarno 1965, p.75f.

Pancasila means “five principles”. Sukarno never claimed to have coined them himself, but, according to him, he found them in the “bog of our own traditions, similar to five wonderful pearls”[144]: “I only *dug it up* from the soil of our Motherland, Ibu Pratiwi. The Political Manifesto was born from the womb of Mother History.”[145] *Pancasila's* five principles need to be seen against the light of the *Gotong-Royong*:

Kebangsaan, nationalism,
Kemanusiaan, humanism or internationalism,
Kerakyatan, representative form of government or democracy,
Keadilan Sosial, social justice,
Ketuhanan, belief in one god[146]

In his 60-minute *Pancasila*-speech on 1 June 1945 Sukarno, for the first time, introduced these principles to his audience.[147] He thereby ended the anxiousness of the “Preparatory Committee of Indonesian Independence” which had been called to life in May 1945 ander the name *Panitia Penyelidik Usaha-Usaha Persiapan Kemerdekaan Indonesia.*
There were mainly two types of factions: the pro-parliamentary and pro-presidential representatives, in favor of a US-based system. And the others preferring a Muslim theocracy. Sukarno as a third faction prevailed with his concept of the *Pancasila* which was included as the preamble to the constitution in 1945.

[144] Sukarno 1965, p.197.
[145] A Year of Living Dangerously Speech, 17. August 1964, quoted in Legge 2003[3], p.357.
[146] Gimonca Homepage w.o.y. Pancasila.
[147] Gimonca Homepage w.o.y. 1940 to 1945.

[148] The *Pancasila* was the way out of the tie between the constitutionalists and the islamists.[149]

Referring to nationalism, Sukarno maintained Indonesia to be a unity, by god's will, of all peoples between Sumatra and Irian. Humanism and internationalism, Sukarno claimed, "must not be *Indonesia über Alles*"[150], but, referring to Gandhi, must be a nationalism in love with humanity. Our nationalism can only grow in the garden of this internationalism.[151] This approach underlines Sukarno's understanding that humankind has certain traits which are the same all over the world and connect human beings from all over the world with each other.[152]

By talking about democracy, Sukarno did not mean a western concept, but the system of negotiation and agreement, the *Permusyawaratan* and the *Mufakat*. In terms of social justice Sukarno opposed the capitalists; he reminded his audience of the *Ratu-Adil*, who now was the symbol of justice in Indonesia's society.

Finally he focused on point five: "Let each worship as he chooses. Let us declare the fifth principle as the civilised way: Belief in one God with mutual respect for one another."[153] By declaring this theistic freedom of religion he clearly negated the way for an islamic theocracy. He was convinced that by

---

[148] Hatta 1981, p.221f.
[149] Schwarz 1999, p.10.
[150] Sukarno 1965, p.198.
[151] Sukarno 1965, p.198f.
[152] See Ricklefs 1993^2, p.31.
[153] Sukarno 1965, p.198f.

separating the state from the religion, the latter would actually be freed.[154]

Sukarno, being the master of symbolism that he was, explained why it had to be five principles: five is the number of commitments in islam, each hand has five fingers, and there are five human senses. What is more, even in *Mahabharata* there were five heros. Hence it only made sense to build Indonesia on five principles.[155]

But this was not the end of Sukarno's number symbolism, as in Java, "all is one". He subsummised the first two principles under socio-nationalism, principles three and four in socio-democracy; only belief remained by itself. Five principles were molten into three, and three into one:

> *„If I press down five to get three, and three to get one, then I have a genuine Indonesian term –* gotong royong. *The state of Indonesia which we are to establish should be a state of mutual co-operation. How fine that is! A* Gotong Royong *state!"*[156]

In a newspaper article, "Sukarno by Sukarno himself", he introduced himself to his people as the mixture of all -isms.[157]

---

[154] See Dahm 1966, p.155 and Schwarz 1999, p.168.
[155] Sukarno 1965, p.198f.
[156] Sukarno, quoted in Legge 2003³, p.211.
[157] Legge 2003³, p.165f.

Dahm comments on this procedure and explains the difference to western thinking:

> *"These three ideas (socio-nationalism, socio-democracy and belief) are in western thought "fundamental terms" and can't be compromised any further. But not for Sukarno, the engineer, who never adopted analytical thinking, the revolutionary, who avoided exactly that which promoted revolution, the agonal principle like temptation, the Javanese, who expected salvation and resolution of all problems by the synthesis which already Aristotle had called "the cause of all errors."*[158]

This notional approach differentiates Sukarno distinctly from other nationalist figures in post-colonial societies. Nevertheless, his ideological building was not complete nor coherent. Sukarno was no analytic and showed contempt for "education à la Rotterdam or Harvard." He accused his opponents of "textbook thinking" - their brains were rotten with western indoctrination of constitutionalism and parliamentary democracy. He was not interested in genuinely philosophic questions or the validity of an argument. What counted for Sukarno was that he would be able to use his argument to defeat an opponent.[159]

---

[158] Dahm 1966, p.265.

[159] Legge 2003[3], p.380f.

Leaving aside the stringency of his arguments Sukarno managed to do one thing with the *Pancasila*. He projected the Javanese Weltanschauung onto a modern territorial state and thus made him come to life. Sukarno hereby positioned himself beyond the line of thought of normal politicians. The reduction of the *Pancasila* to one principle, the *Ekasila*, reflects the Javanese understanding of the cosmos in which all is in balance and at its respective place, in which the *Pendawas* cannot exist without the *Kaurawas.*[160]

While clearly being able to criticise the "theory" of the *Pancasila* we need to keep two things in mind. First we have to thank Sukarno for preventing Indonesia to become an islamic theocracy.[161] And secondly, the goal for which Sukarno had developed this thought. The *Pancasila* was the program that formed the largest island nation of the world out of a huge and loose archipelago. And to do this Sukarno needed unity. And for this unity western terminology does not have an adequate name or phrase.[162] This is the legacy of Sukarno.

---

[160] Legge 2003[3], p.398f.

[161] See Schwarz 1999, p. 10 and Ricklefs 1993[2], p.209.

[162] Dahm 1966, p.260.

The legacy of Sukarno

On the preceding pages we have uncovered the history of Indonesian nationalism. We found several influencing factors: the Dutch did not lend any nationalist formation to their colony. Their biggest influence probably was by using the Malay language as official tongue on the archipelago and hence the Indonesians made Bahasa Indonesia their national tongue. What is more, the Dutch, by applying the Western educational system, helped form a local elite. Some were trained overseas in the Netherlands, others, like Sukarno, received Dutch training in Java. Far more than the Dutch, it was the Japanese who gave opportunity to the Indonesians, under the leadership of Sukarno, to build a national front, an army as well as being promoted into the administration. This was reinforced by several Indonesian groups being formed at that time with the purpose of leading the country into independence. The biggest rift in Indonesian society was between the supporters of an islamic theocracy and those of a nation state. However, the Muslim influence was too weak to prevail - Muslims were fighting among themselves (Modernists v orthodox Muslims) as well as along ethnic line.

The island of Java plays a key role in Indonesia. There are four main reasons for that: first of all, Java is (and always has been) the most populous of all islands, being home to more than 70 percent of all Indonesians. Secondly, as well the Dutch as the Japanese permeation was much stronger in Java than on all other islands. Third, several important influences of colonialism came together in Java and made the urge for national unity and independence stronger here than anywhere else. Java also was home to the son of a Javanese father and a Balinese mother and the leading ideologist and politician of the fight for independence: Sukarno. And last, Sukarno successfully applied Javanese mythology to peacefully unify a very diverse, multi-ethnic, polyglot, multi-religious and multi-insular country into one modern Indonesia. We devoted a lot of our attention to the Javanese mythology and to Sukarno himself, and explained his ideology. The result was the *Pancasila*.

But Sukarno's legacy goes beyond the nation building of Indonesia. In shunning the West as well as the East and encouraging other leaders of the emerging world to create the Non-Aligned Movement, Sukarno tried to position his philosophy and world view on a global scale. To this extent Sukarno was a visionary who wanted the world to become a better place, if only nations would not have to choose between the capitalist, imperialist West and the Socialist and Communist East. He might not have been alone with this world view, but he was a strong advocate. In this sense Sukarno became a tragic figure. While nothing is as powerful as an idea whose time has come, the opposite can be true as well. And the time was against Sukarno. The Cuban Missile Crisis, the Vietnam War, the Domino Theory and the intensification of the Cold War with a nuclear global arms race aimed at the assured mutual destruction all factored in to disallow a huge country like Indonesia to be run by a President who might have underestimated the implications of the mighty PKI, the Communist Party of Indonesia. With more than three million members the PKI was the largest

Communist Party outside the Soviet Union and the P.R. China. Sukarno fell victim to the plans the West had with his country; with introducing *Nasakom*, an acronym consisting of *nasionalisme* (nationalism), *agama* (religion) and *komunisme* (communism) in 1960 he had institutionalised the PKI in his government - an act impossible to undo. In addition, the country had severe economic problems, with inflation running up to 600%, and living conditions for most Indonesians worsened (Sukarno had told the West "to go to hell" with their investments, and economic support from Socialist and Communist countries was barely noticeable). In the aftermath of the alleged coup by the PKI it was easy to scapegoat all alleged or real Communists and go on a killing spree costing the lives of up to 1,000,000 humans. Sukarno's decades-long balancing act as *dalang* between the PKI, the military, nationalist as well as Islamist forces ended in a bloodbath committed by Suharto and the West.

The rape of Indonesia

After the end of World War II and with the foundation of the WTO, the IMF and the World Bank, Western governments established an institutionalised dictatorship of their economic system over the rest of the world. Sukarno was opposed to this form of Western imperialist dominance of newly independent countries, just like his own. As we have laid out in the foregoing chapters, Sukarno's concept of nationalism was meant to be an alternative to the established "Western" and "Socialist / Communist" concepts of his time. Emerging markets had to accept the rules of deregulation, privatisation and investment by foreign powers if they wanted to export their goods to the rich world and become players in a new system called "globalisation." During this process, the political and economic forces of the West acted in complete disregard of the needs of post-colonial societies and their peoples and subjugated them to their own addiction to profit at any price.

A new form of imperialism

It was in the 1980s when neoliberal politicians such as Ronald Reagan in the US and Margaret Thatcher in the UK advocated against the until then (even by the most conservative political parties) accepted Keynesianism; it was the end of the "golden age of controlled capitalism." The deconstruction of existing mechanisms of state control over the flow of international capital was the single biggest factor that would shape the future of the societies of our planet; the decline of the welfare state in the West followed directly and impacts inequality to this day - especially in Anglo-Saxon societies. Reagan, Thatcher and their neoliberal buddies created a new world order by "liberating" state-regulated economies and their peoples. The neoliberal form of imperialism represents a much more dangerous concept than that of the conservative war mongers. The concept of the neoliberals is open-ended by the very nature of their belief that it represents a superior form of life. Globalisation had become the newest form of Western imperialism.

By definition it is the establishment of institutions such as the IMF, the World Bank and the WTO as puppet organisations led by Western governments, predominantly the US, that sets apart the current phase of globalisation from earlier periods. And it is exactly this that anti-globalisation forces around the world today rail against.

The year of living dangerously

On August 17th, 1964, in the annual independence day speech, Indonesian President Sukarno ironically told his citizens that the next year of independence would be the year of living dangerously: "tahun vivere pericoloso", as given in Indonesia-Italian in the original speech. On September 30th, 1965 the words became true. The killing of six senior generals, allegedly by the Indonesian communist party (PKI), and general Suharto's iron-fisted stepping in and creating the mess that followed, was the tipping point for Indonesia. In the aftermath, the future new President Suharto killed an estimated one million of his fellow Indonesians in the biggest holocaust the archipelago has seen. This mass murder by the hands of a ruthless Indonesian leader is bad enough, were it not for the fact that Suharto's coming to power and the subsequent sell out of the country was planned, orchestrated and put in place by Western powers. This stands in stark contrast to what President Sukarno had been working for all his political life.

President Sukarno was the first leader of a post-colonial country to set out a third way for newly independent countries, giving them an option to choose their own future, by being non-aligned to either the West or the East. In 1955 Sukarno invited the leaders of the emerging world to Bandung to take part in the first "Asia-Africa-Conference". The leaders of the majority of humankind gathered on the island of Java and agreed on principles to guide their nations, such as respect for fundamental human rights and the principles of the United Nations Charter, respect for the sovereignty and territorial integrity of all nations, the recognition of the equality of all peoples and the settlement of disputes by peaceful means.

It was clear right from the outset that the West was not willing to accept a third pillar of emerging nations in global affairs. Against the background of an intensifying global Cold War and a very hot war in Vietnam, the US was looking for allies, not non-affiliated nations which might fall into the wrong camp.

How to prevent a domino from falling

In domestic politics Sukarno was balancing a very strong military against the Indonesian communist party (PKI). The PKI at that time was the third largest communist party on the globe (after The People's Republic of China and the Soviet Union) with more than three million members. Especially the rural poor joined the PKI in large masses. For them, the PKI was a vehicle against economic suppression, not to fight a revolutionary war against the existing political system or to join the global force of workers - Indonesia at that time did not have much industrialisation to speak of. But the fact that the PKI was so popular heightened the immense dislike of the CIA and the US government. US President Dwight D. Eisenhower had used the term "domino theory" as early as 1954 to describe his theory that, should one nation in Southeast Asia fall and turn communist, the accepted logic would be that others follow. This of course was not proven but it worked just fine to instigate immense fears in the West and in Western media that all of Southeast Asia would become communist should Vietnam "fall". The same logic later made the argument in favour of a US-backed invasion by the Indonesian government of the small nation of East Timor so much easier: to prevent "another Cuba on the shores of Australia". In 1975, during the Carnation Revolution in Portugal, the Portuguese government had announced plans to pull out of East Timor. This in turn created political space to strive for independence; this strife was lead by the left-leaning Timorese party Fretilin and its coalition partner UDT until civil war broke out. When Fretilin unilaterally declared independence from Portugal, Suharto and his regime labeled the Fretilin government in Dili Communist and invaded the country. In the process the Indonesians killed one third of the 680,000 East Timorese, one of the world's bloodiest holocausts in terms of killed citizens in relation to the whole population of one country. The rape victim had become the rapist.

The Americans and the British worked very closely on several sides to assure that the world believed and accepted that Suharto had just prevented the Indonesian domino from falling, and that Suharto was the chosen one. The British intelligence service created a propaganda division in Singapore with the sole aim of discrediting Sukarno, the PKI and Indonesia under Sukarno. The wheels in the West had set in motion to undo all that President Sukarno had done for his country in the two previous decades: he had given all for his people and their independence; he had even kicked out the IMF and World Bank. Sukarno had told the West to "go to hell" with their loans. By refusing loans and the indebtedness of his country, Sukarno had made himself an enemy of the US. The West under the auspices of the American government was not willing to accept friends who had their own idea of an economic system (an early predecessor to George W. Bush's "you are either with us or against us").

In Suharto the West had now found a partner to bring them back into the country again. In the days and weeks after the coup, the CIA in Jakarta supplied Suharto with a list of 5,000 names of alleged communists; Suharto translated this list into the largest massacre the country has ever seen, and one of the biggest genocides of the second half of the 20th century. The purge ended when one million Indonesians had been killed, many of them Chinese, whom Suharto regarded as “Communist by ethnicity”. The weapons were supplied by the UK and the US. The British military was directly involved in supporting the Indonesian military; the CIA pulled strings behind Suharto’s operations. The US government even secretly supplied Suharto with a communications network to enable the Indonesians to plan, communicate and execute mass murder across the archipelago. The advantage: the CIA and US governments were able to listen in as the frequency was known to the US: they knew exactly what was going on. Former CIA operatives declared that the coup in Indonesia was used as a model version for Operation Phoenix in Vietnam as well as to get rid of President Allende in Chile.

Meanwhile the press in the West never reported about the human catastrophe, genocide and mass killings in Indonesia that were instigated by the British and US-American governments. Nor did the press in the West describe and explain the role of the British and US-American governments and their intelligence services in ousting President Sukarno from power in a staged communist coup. In the aftermath of an Indonesian genocide that left a million human beings dead and the subsequent handover of power from a severely weakened Sukarno to the new President Suharto, the West gathered in November 1967 in Geneva in a conference ironically called “To aid in the rebuilding of a nation." That the Indonesian nation had to be rebuild at all was a circumstance owed to the West.

Indonesia loses her virginity

While the first day of this conference was spent on congratulating Suharto from saving Indonesia from going communist and declaring that "we are trying to create a new climate in which private enterprise and developing countries work together ... for the greater profit of the free world", so James Linen, president of Time Inc., the company that had organised the conference, the second day was spent in cutting up the Indonesian economy and doling out industry sectors to Western organisations. Indonesia had officially lost its virginity. What happened on day two in Geneva is unseen and unheard of and lays the foundation of the unjust principles of globalisation to this very day. The Indonesian citizens are paying the price, and will continue doing so in the future. To this day they are the victims.

The Indonesian economy was cut up into five different verticals: mining, services, light industry, banking and finance, each in a different room. In each room representatives of Western businesses would dictate the representatives of the Indonesian government what they needed in each sector and thereby designed the legal infrastructure of the country. It was the biggest sell out ever forced on a sovereign nation: the Freeport Company received a copper mountain in West Papua, Alcoa got Indonesia's bauxite, others the tropical forests. Suharto, ever thankful for having been swept into power and for being backed by the West, made the first five years tax free. Meanwhile, the real power over the Indonesian economy went to the Inter-Governmental Group on Indonesia (IGGI), consisting primarily of representatives of the US, Europe, Australia, Canada as well as (you might have guessed by now) the IMF and the World Bank.

While Indonesia had basically been debt-free under Sukarno, the country now had millions of dollars in forms of loans from the World Bank rolling in and had become a slave to its dictates. Suharto was in power for more than thirty years. Out of the 30 billion dollars in overall loans by the World Bank to the Indonesian people during this period, an estimated eight billion dollars went directly into the pockets of Suharto, his family and cronies - illegally and by silent consent of the World Bank. While Indonesia had finally disposed of Suharto in 1998 among "krismon", the Asian financial crisis (yet another glorious chapter of Western globalisation of the world), many family members of Suharto as well as friendlies of the former dictator and mass murderer continue owning large parts of the country: highways, airlines, ports, real estate. It is the citizens of the country who are to this day paying the price.

Bibliography

Print

Anderson, Benedict R. O'G. 2003. Imagined Communities: Reflections on the Origin and Spread of Nationalism. London and New York: Verso.

Asian Forum for Human Rights and Development [FORUM-ASIA] (ed.) 1995. Indonesia 50 Years after Independence. Stability and Unity on a Culture of Fear. Bangkok: Asian Forum for Human Rights and Development.

Barley, Nigel 2002. In the Footsteps of Stamford Raffles. London: Classic Penguin, Essential Asia.

Barton, Greg 2002. Gus Dur. The Authorized Biography of Abdurrahman Wahid. Jakarta: Equinox Publishing (Asia) PTE. LTD.

Dahm, Bernhard 1966. Sukarnos Kampf um Indonesiens Unabhängigkeit. Werdegang und Ideen eines asiatischen Nationalisten. Band XVIII der Schriften des Institutes für Asienkande in Hamburg. Frankfurt/M. and Berlin: Alfred Metzner Verlag.

Friend, Theodore 2003. Indonesian Destinies. Cambridge, MA and London, UK: The Belknap Press of Harvard University Presp.

Hatta, Mohammad 1957. The Co-operative Movement in Indonesia. Ithaca, NY: Cornell University Presp.

Hatta, Mohammad 1981. Mohammad Hatta. Indonesian Patriot. Memoirs. Singapur: Gunung Agung.

Legge, J.D. 2003[3]. Sukarno. A Political Biography. Singapore: Archipelago Presp.

Multatuli 1987 [1860]. Max Havelaar Or the Coffee Auctions of a Dutch Trading Company. Translated with notes by Roy Edwards. London: Penguin Books.

Münch-Heubner, Peter L. 2000. Osttimor and die Krise des indonesischen Vielvölkerstaates in der Weltpolitik. Berichte und Studien der Hanns-Seidel-Stiftung e.V. München, Band 82. München: Akademie für Politik und Zeitgeschehen der Hanns-Seidel-Stiftung e.V.

O'Rourke, Kevin 2002. Reformasi. The struggle for power in post-Soeharto Indonesia. Crows Nest, NSW, Australia: Allen & Unwin.

Pilger, John. The New Rulers of the World. London, & New York, Verso 2016.

Pilger, John. Hidden Agendas. London, Vintage 1999.

Pilger, John. Freedom Next Time. London, Black Swan 2007.

Ricklefs, M.C. 1993[2]. A History of Modern Indonesia since c. 1300. Stanford, CA: Stanford University Presp.

Schwarz, Adam 1999. A Nation in Waiting. Indonesia's Search for Stability. St. Leonards, NSW, Australia: Allen & Unwin.

Strassner, Renate 1998. Islam in Indonesien – ein Thema ohne Brisanz? In: Rill, Bern (HG.) 1998. Aktuelle Profile in der islamischen Welt. Berichte und Studien der Hanns-Seidel-Stiftung e.V. München, Band 76. München: Hanns-Seidel-Stiftung, p.313-350.

Sukarno, Ahmet 1965. Sukarno. An Autobiography as told to Cindy Adams. Indianapolis u.a.: The Bobbs-Merrill Company, Inc.

The Economist. July 2nd 2016. Indonesia and the South China Sea. Annoyed in Natuna.

Villiers, John 2000 [w.o.y.]. Weltgeschichte Südostasien vor der Kolonialzeit. Band 18. Übersetzt von Philip W.F. Fleck. Augsburg: Weltbildverlag GmbH.

Winchester, Simon 2003. Krakatoa. The Day the World Exploded: August 27th, 1883. New York: Harper Collins Publishers.

Online

Gimonca Homepage w.o.y. Sejarah Indonesia. An Online Timeline of Indonesian History. Beginnings to 1500: The Old Kingdoms and the Coming of Islam. Electronic document. <www.gimonca.com/sejarah/sejarah01.shtml> [280804]

Gimonca Homepage w.o.y. Sejarah Indonesia. An Online Timeline of Indonesian History.
1830 to 1910: Imperialism and Modernisation. Electronic document. <www.gimonca.com/sejarah/sejarah05.shtml> [280804]

Gimonca Homepage w.o.y. Sejarah Indonesia. An Online Timeline of Indonesian History.
1910 to 1940: New Nationalism. Electronic document. <www.gimonca.com/sejarah/sejarah06.shtml> [280804]

Gimonca Homepage w.o.y. Sejarah Indonesia. An Online Timeline of Indonesian History.
1940 to 1945: Perang Dunia Dua (the Second World War). Electronic document. <www.gimonca.com/sejarah/sejarah07.shtml> [280804]

Gimonca Homepage w.o.y. Sejarah Indonesia. An Online Timeline of Indonesian History.
1945 to 1950: The War for Independence. Electronic document. <www.gimonca.com/sejarah/sejarah08.shtml> [280804]

Gimonca Homepage w.o.y. Sejarah Indonesia. An Online Timeline of Indonesian History.
Pancasila. Electronic document. <www.gimonca.com/sejarah/pancasila.shtml> [280804]

Hillenbrand, Barry TIME 100: AUGUST 23-30, 1999 VOL. 154 NO. ⅞
http://edition.cnn.com/ASIANOW/time/asia/magazine/1999/990823/cia.html

Khalik, Abdul 2003. Separatist movements are main threat to RI, not terrorism. Electronic document. Jakarta: The Jakarta Post Online, December 08, 2003. <www.thejakartapost.com> [081203]

Oppenheimer, Joshua on “The Act of Killing” - The Vice Podcast 034 https://youtu.be/9ibGiP_9Jd8

Szczepanski, Kallie. "Biography of Sukarno, Indonesia's First President." ThoughtCo, Feb. 11, 2020, thoughtco.com/sukarno-indonesias-first-president-195521

The Act of Killing. A movie by Joshua Oppenheimer. 2012. https://youtu.be/-349HTKhPno

The Jakarta Post Online 2004. General Moerdani dies at 74. Electronic document. Jakarta: The Jakarta Post Online, August 29, 2004. <www.thejakartapost.com> [290804]

The Jakarta Post Online 2004. I am ready to become president, says Guruh Soekarnoputra. Electronic document. Jakarta: The Jakarta Post Online, January 19, 2004. <www.thejakartapost.com> [190104]

Toer, Pramoedya Ananta, SOEKARNO, TIME Asia story TIME 100: 23–30 AUGUST 1999 VOL. 154 NO. 7/8, http://edition.cnn.com/ASIANOW/time/asia/magazine/1999/990823/sukarno1.html

Unidjaja, Fadli and Desy, Fabiola 2004. Megawati secures tiny Nipah island. Electronic document. Jakarta: The Jakarta Post Online, February 22, 2004. <www.thejakartapost.com> [220204]